The Confederate Soldier

by Jennifer Blizin Gillis

Content Adviser: Lisa Laskin, Ph.D.,
Department of History,
Harvard University

Reading Adviser: Rosemary G. Palmer, Ph.D.,
Department of Literacy, College of Education
Boise State University

COMPASS POINT BOOKS
MINNEAPOLIS, MINNESOTA

Compass Point Books
3109 West 50th Street, #115
Minneapolis, MN 55410

Visit Compass Point Books on the Internet at *www.compasspointbooks.com*
or e-mail your request to *custserv@compasspointbooks.com*

On the cover: Portrait of Confederate soldiers from Louisiana in 1861

Photographs: Corbis, cover, 4, 10, 12, 14, 16, 19; Prints Old and Rare, back cover (far left); Library of Congress, back cover, 7, 9, 18, 38; The Granger Collection, New York, 5, 21, 26, 27, 35, 39; Chicago Historical Museum, USA/The Bridgeman Art Library, 6; Bettman/Corbis, 11, 13, 15, 17, 22, 29, 34, 36; Hulton Archive/Getty Images, 24; Medford Historical Society Collection/Corbis, 30; Paul A. Souders/Corbis, 32; Snark/Art Resource, N.Y., 37.

Editor: Shelly Lyons
Page Production: Blue Tricycle
Photo Researcher: Abbey Fitzgerald
Cartographer: XNR Productions, Inc.
Library Consultant: Kathleen Baxter

Creative Director: Keith Griffin
Editorial Director: Carol Jones
Managing Editor: Catherine Neitge

Library of Congress Cataloging-in-Publication Data
Gillis, Jennifer Blizin, 1950–
  The Confederate soldier / by Jennifer B. Gillis.
    p. cm.—(We the people)
  Includes bibliographical references and index.
  ISBN-13: 978-0-7565-2025-0 (hardcover)
  ISBN-10: 0-7565-2025-8 (hardcover)
  ISBN-13: 978-0-7565-2037-3 (paperback)
  ISBN-10: 0-7565-2037-1 (paperback)
 1. Confederate States of America. Army—History—Juvenile literature. 2. Confederate States of America. Army—Military life—Juvenile literature. 3. Soldiers—Confederate States of America—Juvenile literature. 4. United States—History—Civil War, 1861–1865—Equipment and supplies—Juvenile literature. I. Title. II. We the people (Series) (Compass Point Books)
  E546.G55 2007
  973.7'42—dc22   2006003989

TABLE OF CONTENTS

WAR!

On November 6, 1860, Abraham Lincoln was elected president of the United States. Many Southerners felt the election had been unfair. There were 23 Northern states and 11 Southern states, so Southerners felt they did not have an equal voice in the country's government.

Slavery was a major issue during the election. Although Lincoln did not call for an end to slavery, he was against the spreading of slavery to the western territories. These territories were places where farmers and their families could build new farms. Some Northerners agreed with

President Abraham Lincoln

4

Lincoln, while others wanted to do more than limit the spread of slavery—they wanted to abolish it completely. Some Southerners, however, owned plantations, or large farms, where enslaved people did the work. The plantation owners thought the Southern economy would collapse if slavery ended.

Plantation owners used slave labor to increase their profits.

Most Southerners did not believe Lincoln when he said he would not abolish slavery in the South. Just one month after Lincoln was elected, South Carolina seceded, or withdrew, from the United States. South Carolina was one of the wealthiest states in the South, and its lawmakers had been threatening to leave the Union for some time. By March 1861, six more states—Mississippi, Florida, Alabama, Georgia, Louisiana, and Texas—also seceded. These states banded together to form the Confederate States of America, and they named Jefferson Davis their president. In time, four more states—Virginia, Arkansas, Tennessee, and North Carolina—would leave the Union.

Confederate President Jefferson Davis

6

The people of the Confederacy worried that the Union would attack the South. They needed soldiers who would fight to preserve slavery and states' rights.

On April 12, 1861, Confederate troops attacked Fort Sumter, in Charleston, South Carolina. This attack marked the beginning of the Civil War.

The attack on Fort Sumter was an early victory for the Confederacy.

The Civil War produced numerous bloody battles and left the South in ruins.

Across the South, men rushed to sign up as soldiers.
Most volunteers had never been far away from home and
thought the war would bring them adventure and glory.

Many thought they would quickly defeat the Union, maybe even after one or two glorious battles.

However, the Civil War raged on for four long years. During that time, about 260,000 Confederate and 360,000 Union soldiers died. Countless families were torn apart, and much of the South was destroyed.

Confederates were ready to fight.

RECRUITING

The Union already had an established Army and Navy. There were military camps to train new soldiers and storehouses full of uniforms and weapons to give them. Because the Confederacy was a new government, it was not as prepared. There was no organized military,

but there were state militias that could be called upon in emergencies. These militias, however, were more like clubs than military units. In most cases, they were not well organized or adequately equipped.

Before the Civil War, some Southerners had served as officers in the U.S. Army. At the beginning of

Confederate soldiers did not always have complete uniforms.

the war, many of them left the U.S. Army to organize the Confederate Army. One of the most famous of these officers was General Robert E. Lee. After spending 22 years in the U. S. Army, Lee was forced to make a choice between his loyalty to the United States and his loyalty to his home state of Virginia. The decision was difficult for Lee, but he chose to join the Confederate Army. Over the course of the war, Lee

General Robert E. Lee and his famous horse, Traveller

led several major Confederate victories, such as the second Battle of Bull Run and the Battle of Chancellorsville.

The second Battle of Bull Run was fought on August 29, 1862.

Most of the men who enlisted in, or joined, the Confederate Army were farmers between the ages of 18 and 29. Usually, they had been born in the South. Confederate soldiers were nicknamed "Johnny Rebs," because they were rebels against the Union. African-Americans were not allowed to enlist and likely would not have wanted to be Confederate soldiers, but early in the war some wealthy soldiers brought enslaved people along to cook and perform chores.

At first, no one younger than 18 could enlist as a Confederate soldier, so many boys lied about their age. There was no age requirement for musicians, so boys as young as 9 years old signed up to be drummers or buglers.

Young boys joined the Army.

The number of new Army volunteers began to fall, so in 1862, the Confederate government passed a draft law. This law meant that all healthy men between the ages of 18 and 35 had to join the Army for three years. By 1864, all Southern men ages 17 to 50 were forced to join. However, plantation owners who held more than 20 slaves were permitted to keep one white male at home. Because of this exception, some Southerners believed the draft was unfair.

13

Confederate soldiers lined up for drill.

Usually, only wealthy men were able to avoid service, while those who had less were forced to join the military and face the possibility of death. More importantly, many Southerners thought the draft violated their rights as citizens.

Despite their concerns, volunteers were eager to fight. Most of them had grown up using guns for hunting,

14

so they thought they knew enough to go right into battle. The men did not see the sense in being told how and when to fire their weapons. The hours of marching and drilling they were forced to do seemed pointless and boring to some.

Soldiers were organized into regiments of 1,000 men. Each regiment was divided into 10 companies of 100

Confederate soldiers of the 3rd Georgia Infantry

Sometimes Confederate soldiers had time to relax in camp.

men each. Companies elected their own officers and chose their own names. Within each company, three or four men formed a small group called a mess, which shared food and chores. Soldiers had at least one messmate, or buddy. Like brothers or best friends, messmates shared food and supplies, helped each other in battle or times of sickness, and wrote a last letter home to a soldier's family or sweetheart

16

to tell where and how the soldier had been killed.

However, men were not the only ones who fought for the Confederacy. Women were not allowed to join the Confederate Army, but there were female soldiers who served. Some Southern women who disguised themselves as men passed the poor medical exams and were able to enlist. Lieutenant

Loreta Janeta Velazquez disguised as Lieutenant Harry J. Buford

Harry T. Buford, whose real name was Loreta Janeta Velazquez, joined the Confederate Army in 1861. When her identity was discovered, she was asked to leave the Army. She re-enlisted and fought in the Battle of Shiloh.

Lucy Matilda Thompson from North Carolina joined the Confederate Army with her husband, Bryant Gauss. Her identity was discovered when she was seriously wounded in the first Battle of Bull Run in 1861.

17

IN CAMP

During the winter months, both Confederate and Union troops set up winter quarters. Officers tried to make sure winter quarters were far away from towns and homes so that soldiers would not be tempted to sneak off and get into trouble. Cold, hungry soldiers often stole food or took

Winter quarters for Confederate soldiers at Manassas, Virginia, in 1862

18

fencing to burn in their campfires at night.

Confederate soldiers were very creative when building shelters for themselves. Some built cabins, complete with wooden walls, roofs, floors, beds, doors, windows, and stone fireplaces. Others built shelters, sometimes called shebangs or

Confederate artillerymen camped at Fort Pemberton, South Carolina, in 1863.

bombproofs, that had four wooden walls, roofs made from tents, and chimneys made from empty barrels. Not all Confederate soldiers had the means to build such luxurious shelters, and as supplies dried up toward the end of the war, they often had no shelters at all. Carlton McCarthy, a soldier in the Army of Northern Virginia wrote, "Two

19

men slept together, each having a blanket and an oil-cloth; one oil-cloth went next to the ground. The two laid on this, covered themselves with two blankets, protected from the rain with the second oil-cloth on top, and slept very comfortably through rain, snow or hail, as it might be."

Though there was plenty of hard work—cutting wood, digging ditches, building roads—there was some free time in camp. Religious study and services often helped pass time. The soldiers also played cards, read, told jokes and war stories, and played baseball or marbles. They had little money, so they gambled their belongings—coats, blankets, extra food—on wrestling matches, races, or other games. Music was also a favorite pastime, and soldiers who played instruments were always among the most popular people in camp. They enjoyed patriotic songs such as *Dixie* or *The Bonnie Blue Flag* and sad songs such as *Home Sweet Home*.

Some of the soldiers even had pets. A group of soldiers from Richmond, Virginia, had a dog named

Stonewall who was taught to line up with them for drills and roll call. A group of soldiers from Mississippi acquired a camel named Douglas who was killed in Vicksburg.

Despite the pleasant activities, camp life could be difficult, too. Arguing, swearing, and drinking took place in camp as the soldiers' tolerances for camp life grew thin.

No matter how much of a relief it was not to be marching, fighting, and sleeping in the open, soldiers

In camp, soldiers made food, relaxed, and prepared for battle.

21

Confederate soldiers in their camp shelter

were still far from their homes and without enough food or clothing to keep them warm. Though they couldn't always depend on deliveries of supplies during times of heavy fighting, there were other ways to get food when the Army was on the move. After a battle, Confederate soldiers often stuffed their haversacks with food from fallen Union

22

troops. They helped themselves to fruits and vegetables in nearby orchards and fields or found chickens, eggs, or pigs to cook. Rummaging around the countryside looking for food was called foraging, but it was just another word for stealing. Soldiers were not supposed to do it, but officers usually pretended not to know about it, because they could not let their troops starve. Some farm families tried to stop the stealing by selling food, though the prices were too high for men who might have gone six months or a year without pay. A dozen eggs could cost as much as $2—worth about $36 in today's money.

Soldiers were supposed to receive standard rations, which meant pork or beef and bread or cornbread every day. They were given cornmeal or flour to bake their own bread. Every so often, soldiers also received dried peas, beans or rice, coffee, sugar, and salt. But resources were stretched too thin, and early in the war, rations were cut back, and soldiers were forced to get by on less.

The Confederate government asked farmers and

23

plantation owners to grow more vegetables and add to their chickens, pigs, and cows so the Confederate Army would be able to buy food locally. But fighting began in April 1861, and crops did not ripen until mid-summer. Moreover, many planters refused to help, preferring to make more money by growing and shipping cotton.

Plantations grew crops such as cotton or tobacco, which brought in much more money than growing food.

By July of 1861, there were already reports of troops near starvation. The Army bought some food from Northern suppliers, imported foods from the Bahamas, and captured some Union food storehouses. Still there was never enough, and the quality was very poor. Soldiers wrote about bugs in the cornmeal and flour. They joked about meat so rotten that they would all be poisoned before the Yankees could get them. Flour, cornmeal, salt, and sugar became moldy in the cold, damp winters.

It was harder to sneak away from winter camp, and there were few food crops to steal. Soldiers often lived on "Confederate Coosh"—cornmeal mixed with a little water or molasses—or "slapjack"—a kind of pancake made with bacon grease, flour or meal, and water. They made coffee with everything from peanut shells to potato skins. One soldier wrote: "Our … horses were supplied with corn and forage, and on several occasions after going twenty-four hours without any food I [stole] the horses' corn … for a meal. … The bacon … when fried and eaten with eyes

25

Confederate volunteers posed before the first Battle of Bull Run in 1861.

shut, and nostrils closed, did no harm."

    The poor diet and lack of warm clothes and shoes were enough to make many soldiers sick, but the conditions in camp were even more dangerous. Soldiers used any nearby creeks or ponds as bathtubs, toilets, and sources of drinking water. They threw garbage outside their doors, and animal waste was left to rot where it fell. They rarely washed, and their hair and clothes were infested with lice.

Living in these conditions, Confederate soldiers often contracted diseases such as typhoid fever, dysentery, diarrhea, and tuberculosis. Many fell sick and died before they ever saw battle. Charlie Baughman, a young soldier in

A Confederate hospital near Sharpsburg, Maryland

27

the 1st Regiment of Virginia, wrote to his mother just six months after the Civil War began: "I left a week ago today to join my regiment and after traveling two days and making only twelve miles, I broke down. … Now dear Ma please do' nt be alarmed for I only broke down from weakness. … I suffered very much too from a pain in my breast, when I walk far. … I cannot draw a long breath without severe pain. … I found out that I also had the Yellow Jaundice."

Doctors had not yet discovered the causes of many diseases or how to keep them from spreading, so it's not surprising that more than half of the 260,000 Confederate soldiers who died during the war did so from disease.

IN BATTLE

Early in the war, most battles took place during the day. Women from nearby towns sometimes came out to watch the action. Fighting stopped just before dark so that each side could take wounded or dead soldiers from the battlefield. But as the war dragged on, there were attacks

The Battle of Gettysburg lasted for three days in July 1863.

after dark. Even in battles lasting more than a day, there were always short bursts of heavy fighting mixed with hours of digging pits and trenches, sitting, standing, or marching around, while waiting for officers' orders to move.

To make attacking difficult for the enemy, soldiers cut and stacked brush and tree limbs so the enemy had to climb over the debris to reach them. If they had more time,

Chevaux-de-frise *were barriers that made attacking the enemy very difficult.*

30

they made *chevaux-de-frise*, which were huge barriers of sharpened tree limbs. As enemy soldiers made their way through these obstacles, they became easy targets.

Battles often began with an artillery barrage. To try to open up gaps for their infantry to break through, field guns from both sides fired at each other. This action could last several hours.

When ordered to do so, infantry soldiers stood shoulder-to-shoulder in lines. They were trained to stay within 13 inches (33 centimeters) of the soldiers in front of them and as close as possible to the soldiers on their left and right. At the call of "charge," they ran forward, following a soldier who carried the battle flag. This soldier was called the standard-bearer.

Each company and regiment had its own flag. This important symbol reminded soldiers of their friends, homes, and families. Flags helped them stay organized in the confusion on the battlefield, but because flags were so important, enemy soldiers often aimed for the standard-bearer

The standard-bearer held the Confederate flag during a
re-enactment of a Civil War march.

first. When one fell, another soldier took up the flag and

led the troops ahead. It was not unusual for a company to

lose several standard-bearers in a single battle.

Going into battle, Confederate soldiers let loose a blood-curdling "rebel yell." This wild combination of a scream and shout scared the enemy, while it helped Confederate soldiers feel braver. One soldier said, "I always said if I ever went into a charge, I wouldn't holler! But the very first time I fired off my gun I hollered as loud as I could, and I hollered every breath till we stopped."

The first row of soldiers fired its weapons, then dropped back to reload and allow the next line of soldiers to fire. Rifles and muskets could only fire one shot at a time, so soldiers had to bite off the end of a paper cartridge, pour the contents down the muzzle of their weapon, push it in with the ramrod, remove the ramrod, then fire. All of this action had to happen within seconds. As men fell, or as the lines of battle changed, men from the rear moved forward to close the gaps.

Cannonballs whistled past and shook the ground as they landed. Gunfire was so loud that soldiers' ears might ring for hours after a battle. Injured men and horses

A cannon in a Confederate embankment was aimed at enemy lines.

screamed as they fell. Smoke from the guns drifted like fog, filling the air with the smell of burning gunpowder and making it difficult for soldiers to see. Soldiers' mouths and faces were blackened from biting open their cartridges of powder.

If the enemy was located in a protected area or on a hill, the fighting could be almost hopeless. At the Battle of Gettysburg in 1863, Confederate soldiers tried to charge Union forces that were located on two hilltops. As the troops fought their way up the hills, waves of Confederates were mowed down. About 28,000 Confederate troops died

34

or were wounded in the Battle of Gettysburg. The Union had 23,000 casualties. These casualties combined made Gettysburg the bloodiest battle of the Civil War.

As the war dragged on, some Confederate soldiers received desperate letters from their families. Some women wrote letters in which they pressured their men to return home and help take care of their homes and families. These women had lost hope. To

A Confederate cavalryman read a letter from home.

them, the importance of saving their families outweighed the importance of winning the war. For this reason, and others, many exhausted Confederate soldiers tried to desert,

35

Rifles and soldiers' bodies lay along the battleground following the Battle of Chancellorsville near Fredericksburg, Virginia, in May 1863.

or run away from, their duties. Some generals ordered officers to stay behind the lines during a battle so they could shoot soldiers who tried to run away. Those who did get away could be hanged or killed by a firing squad if they were caught. If they were able to reach their homes, they had to hide or else run the risk of being turned in by neighbors. By the last year of the war, the choice for most Confederate soldiers was a desperate one and caused many to lose hope.

PEACE

By April 1865, General Robert E. Lee's Army of Northern
Virginia had suffered numerous defeats at the hands
of the Union Army. Many of the soldiers were in poor
health, were hungry, and morale was low. Richmond, the
Confederate capital, had been captured by Union troops,
and Jefferson Davis had escaped, along with the rest of the
Confederate government officials.

Exhausted Confederate soldiers gathered around a Confederate flag.

37

On April 9, the Union Army surrounded Lee's troops at Appomattox Court House, Virginia, and Lee surrendered to Union General Ulysses S. Grant. Although some Confederate troops in the Deep South would keep fighting until the end of May, the Civil War was over. The Confederate soldiers were ordered to turn in their weapons and their battle flags.

Many of the soldiers had not eaten in days, so

General Robert E. Lee (right) surrendered to Union General Ulysses S. Grant at Appomattox Court House, Virginia.

38

Lee and Grant arranged for them to be given food. Eyewitnesses wrote about seeing lines of ragged, starving soldiers placing their weapons in a pile, then squaring their shoulders and saluting the Union troops.

Before they could go home, all Confederate soldiers had to swear an oath of loyalty and promise not to fight against the United States again. Then they were given papers called paroles. These papers allowed them to walk

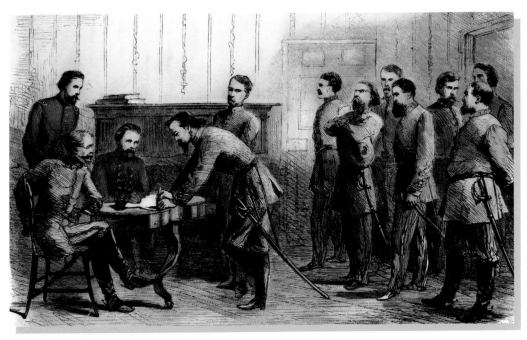

Officers signed paroles for Confederate soldiers to carry on their journey home.

Confederate soldiers had to turn in their weapons before making their way home.

through the countryside without being recaptured by
Union troops.

Getting home was another challenge for the exhausted
Confederate soldiers. Most had no money, and those with

40

Confederate money found that it was worthless. Infantry soldiers made their way home in the same way they had spent the last several years: tired, hungry, and on foot. Cavalry soldiers were allowed to keep their horses, if they still had them.

When the soldiers finally got home, there were no parades or cheery celebrations to welcome them home. A Confederate soldier described fellow soldiers returning to Richmond, Virginia, in 1865: "Silent, friendless, and sorrowful each one went his way. No welcome, no cheer awaited their return to this city and to their homes. … Nothing but ruins everywhere."

GLOSSARY

abolish—to end the observance or effect of

artillery—large guns, such as cannons, that require several soldiers to load, aim, and fire

cavalry—soldiers who are mounted on horseback

Confederacy—the Southern states that fought against the Northern states in the Civil War; also called the Confederate States of America

drilling—exercising or training soldiers in marching and in executing movements with a weapon

infantry—soldiers trained to fight on foot

militias—military forces, often made up of volunteers

muzzle—the discharging end of a weapon

Union—the United States of America: also the Northern states that fought against the Southern states in the Civil War

DID YOU KNOW?

- Cavalry soldiers fought the enemy with pistols and special swords called sabers. Infantry soldiers fired rifles or used attachments called bayonets. Artillery soldiers fired field guns or cannons.

- The cloth for Confederate uniforms was colored with dye made from nutshells, which made it a yellowish-brown instead of a true gray. Union soldiers sometimes called Confederate soldiers "Butternuts" because of this.

- In 1863, President Lincoln issued the Emancipation Proclamation, which freed the enslaved people of the South. The Confederates didn't consider Lincoln their president, so they refused to free their slaves. Only slave owners living in areas occupied by the Union were forced to free their slaves.

- In June 1865, two months after Lee surrendered, the last Confederate general surrendered to the Union. He was Brigadier General Stand Watie, a chief of the Cherokee Nation who commanded a regiment of Creek, Seminole, and Cherokee Indians.

IMPORTANT DATES

Timeline

1860
In November, Abraham Lincoln is elected president of the United States; in December, South Carolina is the first state to secede from the Union.

1861
In February, seven more states secede from the Union and form the Confederate States of America, with Jefferson Davis as president; in April, Confederate troops fire on Fort Sumter.

1863
In January, President Lincoln issues the Emancipation Proclamation; in July, Confederates are defeated at Gettysburg, Pennsylvania, when 25,000 to 28,000 Confederate troops are killed or wounded.

1864
In November, Union General William T. Sherman destroys Atlanta, and his troops begin their March to the Sea.

1865
In April, Confederate General Robert E. Lee surrenders to Union General Ulysses S. Grant at Appomattox Court House, Virginia; President Lincoln is assassinated.

IMPORTANT PEOPLE

JEFFERSON DAVIS (1806–1889)
Senator from Mississippi from 1847 to 1861; president of the Confederate States of America from 1861 to 1865

ULYSSES S. GRANT (1822–1885)
General of the Union Army who accepted Confederate General Robert E. Lee's surrender in 1865; president of the United States for two terms, from 1869 to 1877

ROBERT E. LEE (1807–1870)
Commander of the Army of Northern Virginia; commander of the entire Confederate Army

ABRAHAM LINCOLN (1809-1865)
President of the United States from 1861 to 1865; signed the Emancipation Proclamation in 1863; assassinated by a Confederate sympathizer in 1865

WANT TO KNOW MORE?

At the Library

Anderson, Dale. *A Soldier's Life in the Civil War.* Milwaukee: World
   Almanac Library, 2004.

Crewe, Sabrina, and Michael V. Uschan. *Fort Sumter: The Civil War Begins.*
   Milwaukee: Gareth Stevens, 2005.

McDonald, Archie P. *Primary Source Accounts of the Civil War.* Berkeley
   Heights, N.J.: MyReportLinks.com Books, 2006.

Ratliff, Thomas M. *You Wouldn't Want to Be a Civil War Soldier!: A War
   You'd Rather Not Fight.* New York: Franklin Watts, 2004.

Smolinski, Diane. *Soldiers of the Civil War.* Chicago: Heinemann
   Library, 2001.

On the Web

For more information on the *Confederate Soldier*, use FactHound
to track down Web sites related to this book.

1. Go to *www.facthound.com*

2. Type in this book ID: 0756520258

3. Click on the *Fetch It* button.

Your trusty FactHound will fetch the best Web sites for you!

On the Road

**Pamplin Historical Park and the
National Museum of the Civil
War Soldier**
6125 Boydton Plank Road
Petersburg, VA 23803
Interactive exhibits about soldiers'
daily lives as well as walking trails
along the original earthworks

The Museum of the Confederacy
1201 East Clay St.
Richmond, VA 23219
Exhibits and photographs from
the Confederacy

Look for more We the People books about this era:

The Assassination of Abraham Lincoln
ISBN 0-7565-0678-6

Battle of the Ironclads
ISBN 0-7565-1628-5

The Carpetbaggers
ISBN 0-7565-0834-7

The Dred Scott Decision
ISBN 0-7565-2026-6

The Emancipation Proclamation
ISBN 0-7565-0209-8

Fort Sumter
ISBN 0-7565-1629-3

The Gettysburg Address
ISBN 0-7565-1271-9

Great Women of the Civil War
ISBN 0-7565-0839-8

The Lincoln-Douglas Debates
ISBN 0-7565-1632-3

The Missouri Compromise
ISBN 0-7565-1634-X

The Reconstruction Amendments
ISBN 0-7565-1636-6

Surrender at Appomattox
ISBN 0-7565-1626-9

The Underground Railroad
ISBN 0-7565-0102-4

The Union Soldier
ISBN 0-7565-2030-4

Women of the Confederacy
ISBN 0-7565-2033-9

Women of the Union
ISBN 0-7565-2035-5

A complete list of We the People titles is available on our Web site:
www.compasspointbooks.com

INDEX

About the Author

Jennifer Blizin Gillis writes poetry and nonfiction books for children. She first became interested in the Civil War while living near Fredericksburg, Virginia, close to many battlefields. She lives on a former dairy farm in Pittsboro, North Carolina, with her husband, a dog, and a cat.